Love Me, Love My Cat!

Written & Illustrated by Keith Robinson

BOWTIE
P R E S S

Irvine, California

Karla Austin, Business Operations Manager
Jen Dorsey, Editor
Michelle Martinez, Associate Editor

Rebekah Bryant, Editorial Assistant
Ruth Strother, Editor-at-Large
Nick Clemente, Special Consultant

Library of Congress Control Number: 2004101937
ISBN 1-889540-67-6

BowTie Press®
A Division of BowTie, Inc.
3 Burroughs
Irvine, California 92618

Printed and Bound in Singapore
10 9 8 7 6 5 4 3 2 1

CONTENTS

INTRODUCTION

Okay, so you don't have a cat. It isn't a crime. Maybe you're allergic. Maybe you're not, as we say, a "cat person." Whatever. It's your life.

You may find a relationship with a cat unavoidable at some point. Your new romantic interest may share a home with a tabby cat. Your best friend might take in strays. Your own child may beg for a kitten. It might seem to you that everyone has a cat and that you have no choice but to jump on the bandwagon.

Humans and cats have coexisted for thousands of years. Ultimately, the only way to stay away from cats is to stay away from people, becoming a recluse holed up in a cabin wearing Kleenex boxes on your feet. Face it. If you are going to lead a normal life, eventually you'll have to deal with the ultimatum, "Love me, love my cat!" The root of your avoidance will determine how you deal with this—practical ("I'm allergic."), apathetic ("I'm not a cat person."), or emotional ("I hate cats!"). But deal with it you can. You need not die alone.

"I'm Allergic"

So why have you been avoiding cats? Maybe, like many people, you're allergic. If so, you've probably discovered that some cat lovers take it as a personal insult if you are allergic to cats.

"I like cats," you say, "but I'm allergic."

"They have shots for that," the cat lover replies in a tone that makes you wonder: *vaccines—or bullets?*

You should learn *never* to say, "Cats make me sneeze." Rather, say, "I'm allergic to cats." The former is seen as blaming the cats.

The latter puts the blame where the cat lover rightly sees it: on you, the miserable sufferer. In spite of your watery-eyed suffering, many cat owners like to point out, "So what?" An estimated 30 percent of cat owners are actually allergic to their own pets, which sounds downright masochistic. The divorce rate might be lower if spouses were willing to put up with that much suffering.

But the truth is, if you are allergic to cats you can take steps to live comfortably among them. You can:

- change the surroundings;
- change the cat;
- change yourself.

Change the Surroundings

Your sympathetic friends will promise, "I'll keep Fluffy locked in a back room for the evening so you won't sneeze." Such people are apparently in denial about the by-products of living with a cat. The average cat-inhabited house has enough shed hair on the furniture and carpet to knit two or three more kittens. Just because you can't see Fluffy doesn't mean you are safe from an allergy attack. So, since you're going to wind up sneezing anyway, you might as well play with the cat. Locking up the cat causes the suffering without the fun.

Some friends knock themselves out, vacuuming every square inch of their home just before you come over. This is extremely thoughtful.

It also, in many cases, makes things worse. The cat hair itself is not what you are allergic to, but a couple of proteins found in cat saliva and on dander (the too-cute name given to the microscopic scales of dried, shed skin, and fur) are what make you sneeze. Saliva left on shed cat hair can be removed by vacuuming up the hair, but unless the vacuum cleaner has a very good environmental, High Efficiency Particulate Air (HEPA) filter, it will fill the air with the microscopic skin particles, creating an invisible cloud of allergens that can linger for hours.

If your friends are going to vacuum, it should be the day before you arrive, giving that cloud a chance to settle. You can pass this info along to your friends, but be careful. People can't help but be annoyed when you start telling them how they should clean their houses. And remember: vacuum cleaners, even with the most advanced HEPA filters, never make good Christmas, birthday, or anniversary presents. You've been warned.

As you become more comfortable visiting friends with cats, you will likely become open to dating someone with cats. One day, you may find yourself in an honest-to-goodness relationship with a cat owner. And this relationship may bloom to the point where you are ready to live with a cat owner and, ergo, one or more cats.

This living arrangement can work by creating an environment that helps decrease the allergens. The main thing is to avoid

fabrics—no carpets, no drapes, no upholstered furniture. Think airport terminal! All right, the minimalist approach may put a strain on the relationship, but a few compromises such as hardwood floors and a leather sofa will help you cope. It also helps to designate one room—particularly the bedroom—as a cat-free zone. This is an excellent idea that in practice will last about a week.

Change the Cat

Can you make a cat hypoallergenic? Well, the proteins you are allergic to are generated by the cat to help her clean herself. Theoretically, if you bathe a cat weekly in warm water, after about

three months the cat will naturally stop producing the proteins and will be hypoallergenic. This is theoretical because, in actuality, it's unlikely that anyone has ever managed to wash a cat once a week for anything close to three months and lived to tell about it. The bottom line is researchers have not been able to prove that bathing, diet, or any over-the-counter treatment can affect a cat's protein output.

Life would be so much easier, you think, *if I didn't have all this cat hair floating around.* Be careful what you wish for. If your kid is begging for a cat, don't get a Sphinx (a hairless breed that looks like a newborn bat) thinking that no hair equals no sneezing. A Sphinx will still leave dander with the protein everywhere, and the cat might creep out your friends, making it difficult for you to find someone to play with her while you're on vacation.

So what can be done to change the cat if you can't swap out one cat for another? Regular brushing helps, and a veterinarian can treat excessive dry skin and flaking. But again, use tact when telling friends how to groom their cats.

Change Yourself

People with allergies believe that if you release a cat into a room full of strangers, the cat will quickly gravitate to the one person who is allergic. While this may sound like an old wives' tale (aka a paranoid delusion), the cat expert will say that this behavior has a basis in reality. The reasoning goes like this: The people in the room who want to pet a cat will look at her and reach for her. The cat perceives both of these actions as threats and she avoids those people. But, says the cat expert, a person who is allergic to cats tends to ignore the furry feline in the hope that she will leave him or her alone. The cat sees this person as nonthreatening—a potential friend—and she scampers right over. So, says the cat expert, stare at the cat, and the cat will keep her distance.

Try it the next time you encounter a cat. Fix her with your most threatening stare. More than likely, she will bound over to you and rub against your leg, purring. This raises the question: just what qualifications does it take to be a "cat expert"? Apparently, knowing anything about cats isn't one of them.

So how can you change your behavior to lessen your allergic reactions? Consider cats to be radioactive. Everything that comes in contact with them and their

environment must be decontaminated at once. If you can't resist petting a cat, only use one hand and consider that hand contaminated. Do not touch anything else on your body with that hand—especially your face—until the hand can be washed and/or boiled.

Dating a cat lover can be a big problem since you might find yourself allergic to their clothing as well as their home. After returning from the home of a cat owner, your clothing should be washed—or preferably burned—immediately. If you don't wash a pair of pants you wore to a cat lover's house and put on that same pair of pants three months later, you'll start sneezing. Laying any of those clothes on your bed can cause nighttime congestion.

Sitting on your sofa after coming home without changing will make you allergic to your sofa. The cycle is vicious, and it's worse than Ebola.

There is also the problem that you can have an allergic reaction when you are with your paramour away from her home and cat. It's important to reassure her that you are allergic to the cat dander on her clothing—not to her. However, explaining that you are allergic to a woman's clothes is not a successful way to get her to remove them.

Thankfully, there are a number of drugs on the market that will lessen your allergic reaction. Many over-the-counter medications

cause drowsiness. It defeats the purpose of taking a pill to visit a cat-owning friend if you wind up passed out and drooling on the couch shortly after arriving. So, use caution when choosing a medication. Several prescription drugs (and some that have been recently approved to be sold over-the-counter) are available that don't cause drowsiness, but they are considerably more expensive. Most need to be taken daily to be effective. At these prices, you may want to get your own cat just to feel the cost is justified.

If you are going to be moving in with a cat owner, you probably will want to ask your doctor about pills or even allergy shots. Your doctor will most likely advise you first and foremost to get rid of the cat. *Do not* relay this advice to your loved one; you will only wind up looking for a new doctor. Rather, chuckle appreciatively, tell the Doc, "That's a good one," and then ask about your medical options.

If you do wind up living with a cat despite your allergies, don't look for sympathy from cat lovers. They'll just sneer, "You'll get used to it," which, in many cases, is true. Many allergy sufferers build up immunities after living with cats; symptoms can lessen or disappear altogether without drugs. If this happens to you, remember: *Keep it to yourself!* By no means should you tell anyone this terrific secret. You can have all the fun of playing with

Fluffy, but when it's time to comb for fleas or empty the litter box or clean up the hairballs—oops, you feel an allergy attack coming on. Just don't overdo it. Also remember that you are always expendable—the cat isn't.

"I'm Not a Cat Person"

Maybe you're not allergic. You simply don't consider yourself a "cat person." Why not?

- **"Cats don't do anything."**

  This is a common complaint of non-cat people, especially those who identify themselves as "dog people." They want a pet who will come when called, do tricks, and protect the house. If you fall into this category, I have two words for you: control freak. You need to be in charge, don't you? Even your pet has to obey you, snapping to order like a new recruit in boot camp. You need to lighten up. And no one can show you better how to lighten up than a cat. Call the cat. The cat doesn't come. Examine the situation. Did you really *need* the cat at that moment? Can't it wait till later? Relax.

Try to teach the cat a trick. The cat stares at you a moment, then wanders off to keep an eye on the piece of paper on the kitchen floor. Examine the situation. Was the trick really that clever? And why is there a piece of paper on the kitchen floor?

A burglar breaks into your house and steals your VCR. The cat slept through it. Examine the situation. Aren't you too tied to material goods? Do you really need a VCR? A nap *does* sound pretty good right now, doesn't it?

Hang out with a cat, and before you know it, you'll be broken of all your control freak habits. You'll *be* a cat person.

- **"Cats destroy a home."**

We all know a cat owner who lives in a home where the furniture is shredded, the rug is stained, and it smells like a litter box. This reflects poorly on the cat. It's not the cat's fault—the owner is a slob. The house would have shredded furniture, a stained rug, and smell like a litter box even if the person didn't own a cat. The cat is just an excuse.

Many people maintain perfectly respectable homes even though a cat lives there. Litter boxes can be kept clean, enzyme-based cleaners can remove spots and smells from carpets, and cats can be trained to use scratching posts and to keep off furniture. And on the other hand, so what if the cat destroys your oh-so-precious couch? Maybe she's just trying to tell you you're too concerned with material things. (See point 1, above.) So what have we learned? If your house is a mess, blame the cat. (Having a cat isn't even necessary—tell visitors she's hiding under the bed.)

- **"Cats are evil."**

Over the centuries, a lot of mythology has developed around cats. They are gods. They are associated with witchcraft. They steal babies' breath. They're bad luck. They hate Mondays and eat lasagna.

Even if you aren't superstitious, it's hard not to be influenced by all the folklore. You are sitting there, minding your own business, when out of the corner of your eye you spot a cat nearby, just sitting and staring at you. What is she plotting? What is she thinking?

She's probably just thinking, "What's that in your hand? Is it food? Is it for me?"

People who fear cats simply don't know cats. Anyone who has lived with cats knows there's nothing supernatural about them, even if they *can* see invisible moths and mice that you can't and obey voices that you can't hear commanding them to suddenly run in or out of the room. But cats are not evil. (The Broadway musical *Cats*, on the other hand just *might* be evil.)

"I Hate Cats"

All right. You're not allergic. And more than just not being a cat person, you insist that you simply hate cats. Now, come on, is that rational? Even at their most destructive, cats aren't really hateable. There must be something deeper. Maybe a kitty bit you when you were a child. Maybe a playground bully named Katz took your lunch money.

Possibly you need a little therapy to see where this anger is coming from. If you don't deal with this, you are dramatically limiting your pool of potential mates. Are you willing to risk being alone for the rest

of your life just to avoid confronting your irrational hatred of cats?

Okay, maybe you can put an ad in the paper or on the Internet to find someone who hates cats as much as you do. Maybe you'll meet someone. Maybe you'll fall in love. The two of you can get married and live in feline-free bliss. And then someday you have a child—a sweet little girl whom you adore and would do anything for. And one day she shows up at the door, her arms full with a big fluffy cat, saying "He followed me home! Can we keep him, Mommy? Can we keep him, Daddy? Pleeeeeease?"

So what do you do now, cat hater? Are you really prepared to break a little girl's heart? Get some help now before it's too late.

Life with Cat People

You've decided you can deal with being around a cat, but can you deal with being around a cat person? If you are going to have a relationship with a cat person, you must be aware that they have idiosyncrasies that you will have to get used to. You may find it easier to get used to a cat than a cat person.

Count the Cats

You may be able to fit this person into your life, but can you fit you into hers? The first clue is, how many cats does your loved one have?

- One cat most likely shows a natural desire for companionship. It shows responsibility and a nurturing nature. Having a single cat may also indicate a person who forms strong individual bonds; a person ready to commit to you if you could just get over your own tendency to be a selfish loner.

- Two cats often reflect a person with a fun-loving and sharing personality; someone who enjoys watching cats play together without feeling left out. It may show concern: not wanting a single cat to be lonely while your loved one is at work, or introducing a younger cat into the household to help keep an older cat frisky.

(Warning to men: do not try to extrapolate her concern for cats to your relationship. Few girlfriends will appreciate you bringing over a younger woman to help keep *them* frisky. Go figure.)

- Now, three cats should set off warning bells. Possibly this person, like the person with two cats, simply enjoys the fun and companionship. But having three cats may well indicate an irreversible trend, meaning this person is just one step away from being . . . a crazy old cat lady. Let's face it, people with four or more cats are crazy old cat ladies, whether or not they are old and whether or not they are female. They've put all of their emotions into cats. After all, cats never betrayed them. A cat never ran off with the pool boy, or the checkout girl, or grew up and moved out and never writes. Obviously, it will take a lot of work to make someone who only trusts cats trust you. He or she had better be worth it. And there are many terrific crazy old cat ladies out there, men and women of all ages. But be forewarned, if the relationship ever ends—no matter if it's after three weeks or thirty years—they'll turn to the cats and say, "See? I told you so!"

Especially beware of the obsessive-compulsive cat person! While most cat lovers can integrate their feline charges into a balanced life, the obsessive-compulsive lives and breathes cats. This person collects everything that has a cat theme. It usually starts innocently enough: seeing a porcelain cat in a store that looks just like Fluffy back home. This grows into a porcelain cat collection then spills over into cat-patterned plates, return address labels, checks, throw pillows, napkins, and bumper stickers. The kitchen, the bedroom, even the bathroom overflows with cats. The real ones tend to get lost in the camouflage.

If you wind up living with this person, it will become your way of life, too. There are advantages: it makes choosing a gift for your loved one a piece of cake. But do you really want to live in Kitty Cat Land? And what may seem cute or innocently obsessive seems less

funny once you have joint bank accounts and credit cards. "You spent $200 on *what*?"

- Beware of the person who uses a cat as a child substitute. How can you tell the difference between a pet and a child substitute? If your loved one has a framed picture of the cat on his or her desk at work, if he or she throws a birthday party for the cat, if the cat is in the will—chances are the cat is a child substitute. This is fine, but just remember that people with a child substitute usually want to substitute a child for the child substitute as soon as possible.
- Does your loved one take in strays? That's a sign that he or she has a big heart or, in other words, is a sucker. If you move in,

expect deadbeat friends and relatives to be living on your couch. On the plus side, if you lose your job you'll know that you can stay pretty much rent-free forever while "looking" for a new one.

- Beware of the person who gets another cat every time a relationship fails. Essentially, this is a crazy old cat lady with baggage.

How Does She Treat the Cat?

You should watch very closely how your loved one treats his or her cat. Does the cat get premium cat food or whatever is on sale? When the cat cries does she get attention—or kicked out of the way? Has your sweetie declawed the cat to protect the furniture? Then beware

the first time you should forget to use a coaster! You might be banished to the garage. Has he or she put a bell on the cat's collar to "always know where she is"? Then forget about going to Vegas alone for the weekend with your old college pals. When the vet says the cat needs a $1,000 operation, does your loved one tearfully say, "Whatever it takes?" or does he or she hesitate, figuring they don't give away flat-screen TVs for free at the pound.

On the one hand, if you are in this person's life, that $1,000 can quickly turn into OUR $1,000. You might see that vacation you had planned or that big screen TV you were set to buy disappear to treat Fluffy. On the other hand, what if you get sick? Do you want your

loved one dumping you at the first sign of your being a burden? Remember that before long, this is how *you* will be treated in your relationship—if you're lucky. A special note for men: you should *not* read anything into it when your girlfriend gets her male cat fixed. Assuming, that is, that she doesn't cackle maniacally as they head off for the vet.

Of course, if the cat is treated substantially better than you, you may want to reexamine your relationship. If you can't go on a romantic weekend because the cat can't be left alone or if your loved one remembers the cat's birthday but not yours, it may be time to move on.

Getting Along

All right, you have decided this person is worth it. You want to hang around. So you'll have to get along with his or her cat. You may be ready for this, but Kitty may not. Cats are not crazy for change, and they'll let you know it.

Many cat owners believe they can communicate with their pets, but no one is exactly sure just what is going on in kitty's brain at times like these. Since we can't know exactly, let's assume it's something like the stages of grief Dr. Elisabeth Kubler-Ross described in

her seminal work, *On Death and Dying*: denial, anger, bargaining, depression, and acceptance.

Denial

The cat may initially choose to ignore you. You don't exist; you aren't there; nothing has changed. The cat will not make eye contact with you the same way he will not make eye contact with himself in a mirror. Nothing to see here; move on.

Anger

When the cat can no longer pretend you aren't there, he may turn to anger. In your efforts not to be ignored and to be friendly, you try to pet Kitty. You wind up getting hissed at and scratched for your trouble.

Bargaining

After Kitty takes a few swipes at you, your loved one will probably start yelling at the cat, scolding him. Realizing that the owner is not on his side, he may start acting up in ways other than directly attacking you, such as scratching furniture and soiling carpets. This may appear to be a continuation of the anger, but it's actually bargaining. Essentially, kitty is saying, "I'll stop this behavior if you get rid of that thing that offends me." That thing, of course, would be you. If your loved one chooses *not to* get rid of you at this point, congratulations—you've passed a major hurdle.

Depression

Once Kitty realizes you're not going anywhere, he may slip into a depression. Kitty may stop eating or become listless. Your sweetie needs to spend plenty of time with the cat, just the two of them, to reassure kitty that he is loved.

Tolerance

With patience and time, the cat's attitude toward you can shift from loathing to tolerance. Now, tolerance is not one of the stages recognized by Kubler-Ross, but it is one that will be recognized by anyone who has disrupted a cat's life. In the tolerance stage, the cat will sit in the same room with you, but he will watch your every move. No matter what you do, the cat will make it known by his squint-eyed stare that he isn't happy about it. "You're sitting in my chair. Who told you that you could sit there? This isn't right. Fix it. Fix it NOW."

A cat can get quite attached to an owner, and quite jealous. When you cuddle up with your loved one, the cat may jump up and try to squeeze between you. Or he may disappear into another room and start noisily pushing things off a table—anything to break up the action. You may be tolerated, but you definitely are not accepted.

Again, Kitty needs reassurance that he is loved and is not being replaced. Kitty's routine must be respected, and you are going to have to be a part of that routine. Kitty must realize that you are going to be part of his care and feeding—in other words, his servant. You must be willing to wait on kitty's every desire. And once Kitty realizes this, he may move to the final stage, acceptance.

Acceptance

Kitty now sees you as part of the household. He butts against you with his head, rubbing a scent from his cheeks to your leg, which says to other cats, "Mine!" He is comfortable when you cuddle with your loved one—he may go cuddle with one of his toys. When he looks at you now it is with relaxed eyes, and when you enter a room he may roll on his back—a sign of trust.

And if you're lucky, he just may curl up in your lap and go to sleep purring because all is right with the world.